By *Eleanor Ross Taylor*

WILDERNESS OF LADIES   *1960*

WELCOME
EUMENIDES

THE BRAZILLER SERIES OF POETRY
Richard Howard, General Editor

WELCOME EUMENIDES

POEMS BY

Eleanor Ross Taylor

with a note by Richard Howard

GEORGE BRAZILLER

New York

Some of these poems have previously appeared in the following publications, to whose editors grateful acknowledgment is made: *The Sewanee Review, Poetry, The Kenyon Review, Southern Poetry Review,* and *The Greensboro Review.*

"Welcome Eumenides," "Eightieth Birthday," "Chapter and Text" appeared in *The Sewanee Review;* "Victory" in *The Kenyon Review;* "After Twenty Years," "Painting Remembered," "Mother's Blessing," "We Are the Fruit," "Cemetery Statue," "His Wishes," "Bulletin," "Pause in Flight," "The Skipped Page" in *Poetry;* "The Guard Remembers," "Don't Leave Hungry," "Song" in *Southern Poetry Review;* "The Wedding Guests," "The Dead," and "History Plan" in *The Greensboro Review.*

Standard Book Number: 0-8076-0644-8, cloth
0-8076-0633-2, paper
Library of Congress Card Number: 73-184877
First Printing
Printed in the United States of America
Designed by Harry Ford and Kathleen Carey

Contents

ELEANOR ROSS TAYLOR

"After you I go, my life! Was it chase or flight?"

In Castalia, not far from where I was raised in northeast Ohio, there is a place called The Blue Hole, which I used to be taken to see as a child: it is a small pond, apparently without source or outlet, blue indeed and said to be bottomless—there is the inevitable story of the team of horses accidentally driven into it one winter night a century ago and never found, though grappled for at unimaginable depths. The Blue Hole is a mysterious site, nor can its mystery be vulgarized, even in northeast Ohio where windshield souvenirs attest your visitation, for there is a silence about this body of water (the expression seems only justice, for once), an unexpected presence from below that keeps the gum-wrappers from polluting such fountains with which poetry has always been associated, as the name Castalia itself reminds us. Of course The Blue Hole is not really bottomless, merely the sudden surfacing, among trivial mediations, of an underground river which then vanishes once more; the team of horses cannot be dragged to the surface because it has been carried away, perhaps the skeletons, or, who knows—say the water is a marinade and the team entire, rolling eyes, streaming manes and tails—will reappear the next time this subterranean source remounts, abstergent, unplumbed, clear, giving back whatever it took into itself.

This natural miracle is before us—it has occurred in the work of Eleanor Ross Taylor. A dozen years ago her first book of poems, *Wilderness of Ladies*, was published with a brilliant introduction by Randall Jarrell "to make it easier for the readers to consider the possibility of the poems' being what they are"; what they are, as our great poet-critic exulted, is a world, like Hardy's or Janacek's, "the water/meeting me around the curve . . . the waiting womb! the waiting tomb—the empty antique sitting room!"—precisely, birth, life, and the process that divides and unites them. Now, after long silence, we are given that speech again, "etched with inheritance and fate," eager yet reticent, reckless and still patient, solicitous, attentive, nursing (it is capital that one of the major pieces here is a dramatic reverie uttered by Florence Nightingale, a poem which gives the book its startling title).

I think Jarrell's prose did make it easier for readers, but perhaps it became harder for the poet, after such praise, such precision ("the world is a cage for a woman, and inside it the woman is her own cage . . . life is a state of siege, a war to the last woman"), to surface again, to welcome the Eumenides which are, we must remember, not the Erinyes, the Furies, but the Kindly Ones, mediators of ritual, functionaries of acceptance.

This new book of Mrs. Taylor's is our fortunate particular and proof that what had seemed a singular welling-up, an exceptional outpouring, is more for being carried on, for returning to observable earth, not just The Blue Hole but a longer look at what Matthew Arnold calls "the unregarded river of our life." We have watched, or at least we have waited, for that American talent which would seal the pact between Emily Dickinson and Walt Whitman, between that private extremity which is a crying need and that public extremity which is an inward wound. And here, with this second collection which includes "A Few Days in the South," the best poem since Whitman about the War Between the States, here is that talent, that reconciliation ("fever, flesh, ash into ashes burn") which is of course a new aggression, a new demand. It is a demand upon the poet herself, an insistence that she come to terms with her resources, with her impoverishment, and it reminds us that Eleanor Ross Taylor is the wife of Peter Taylor, one of our finest narrative writers to concern himself with the voice of a region, the vision of a class, the vaunt of a generation. It is a great thing for a poet to be married to a great prose writer, for his achievement shows her what she must keep overcoming in order to become what she is: a diction out of the shadows which does not erase itself as it is raised. Whereas the prose voice rubs itself out as it goes along, *her* voice must be somehow suspended, held up on its rhythms, its intervals, its silences, until no message is left but a resonance, no communication but an echo: persistent, yielding, heard.

Lest I, too, seem to outspeak Mrs. Taylor who is quite likely to sink back into her garden ("earth to earth, inside you yet/in the garden to come"), the buried stream proceeding to its next unpolicied embodiment, I would not claim for her more than her own purpose, so aptly asserted by her title. *Welcome Eumenides* (the diary notation of Florence Nightingale) is a rehearsal of what Jane Harrison means, in her famous chapter of the *Prolegomena*, "The Making of a Goddess," when she describes the growth of a function from imprecation and warding-off to acceptance and nourishment (nursing!) to welcoming and prayer. That is why the word *attendance* holds both the word for shelter and the word for tension within its etymon, and why, magnificently, Eleanor Ross Taylor will say—it is the way to read her, to let her reveal herself—

> Our language exists but in silence,
> Our mortality in immortality.

RICHARD HOWARD

Brother, we must converse somehow.
Given but the hour,
Juxtaposed thus,
It seems only human.
Yet how to key your tongue
So like the hieroglyphics of your stare,
A seam, a clef, a stamen—
How wreak on silence your mute voice,
How smoke your blind face from the asterisks?
I fear you, stabbed dragon.
I understand the snarl, born of the word.
I pity you, winged jackass in the leaves.
Oh, I despair of myself
That your Berlitz is too simple for me.

     Yet, when you lie across the bed,
Eyes shouting at the ceiling,
Hand clenching letters out of all syntax—
I see what you mean.
Our language exists but in silence. . . .
Our mortality in immortality.

AFTER TWENTY YEARS

After twenty years in France
Do you dream in French, my son? . . .
Home . . . ça existe encore.
Still, still exists Flagg Bros. store,
With new glass front, but behind
The dilapidated sheds
And packed road lined with maypops
Where you talked to the white horse.

Gloved, hatted, I kneel here
Where you by the sky-blue windows
Sang "Onward Christian Soldiers."
For I have needed pardon
Since the morning we found Dad
In the garage (It is hard
To be a father without
A son). I screamed, and without
A son to be a widow.
Shall I pray your pardon too?
Prince of Peace, absolve all warriors,
My warrior of the bow and arrow.
Your old girl married money.
She's grown stout. (*He* has ulcers.)

Last year they were in Nice
Not Normandy. . . .
My glove's rouge, with lipstick
Or with teeth. . . . Curse *men*, curse *free*—
God vault your freedom!

Oh the acres of undistinguished
Crosses make me sick.
Mother could mark Papa's grave
In the churchyard a mile from home,
By its firs and shaft. . . .
Your nothing grave . . .
                          Shame!
God I am of little understanding. . . .
But with God all things are possible. . . .
Give my son another life—
A Norwood ugliness, a bourgeois rot,
Dust and concrete, Falcons and Mustangs, not . . .

MESSAGE TO CAPTOR,
HIGHER ORDER

Why hold me in your hot hot hands?
I find heat nauseating;
This weird celestial trip
Hurtling along past bursting stars
Pains my slow heart
That longs for its clay hole
Unfired by gods.

MOTHER'S BLESSING

This timeless blood was here before *begat*.
    Infinity runs in your veins—
        Not mine, not yours,
            Nor Eve's, nor Adam's—
                Gat of God,
                    And spinning like taffy Godwards back again.
Sapped through the centuries to us,
    Grafting a limb there for the Jesse tree,
        Remultiplied infinitely,
           From heart to heart tick-pulsed,
              Ill clad, ill fed, ill fit—
Here, child, do what you can with it.

THE GUARD REMEMBERS

Only a scullery maid
Running through the garden, sire,
Shoes in hand, cheeks white, her eye
Glittering as an hourglass. . . .

Time flies. . . .
At court the accent nowadays
Is countrified. Law speaks
In some magic of the king's bride:
In each oppressed face he meets
The imperial blue eyes by his side.

WELCOME EUMENIDES

*"God called me in the morning and asked
me would I do good for Him, for Him
alone without the reputation."*

F.N. March 7, 1850

Who calls?
Speak, for thy servant heareth. . . .

Is it the wards at Scutari?
Or the corridors at Waverly,
Where last night eighty slept.
Our masks—my pink gown with black lace—
Moving, at five, exhilarated,
Weary from dancing, up the famous stairs. . . .

Mother!   Nurse!   water! . . .
I come!

But now at five they have not slept
Except the men, heads blanketed, who crept
To timeless shadow.
Two thousand deathbeds that one winter.
Last May my window gave
On a thousand Turkish flowers,
Two thousand English graves.
Two thousand deathbeds that one winter—
Who thinks of that now?

Who calls?
Not my child
(*O God no more love
No more marriage*)
Only my British Army.

7

(Dear Aunt Mai, kiss all babies for me.)
  Oh my poor men I am a bad mother
  To come home and leave you to your Crimean graves.
  73 percent in 8 regiments in 6 months
  From disease alone. (Who thinks of that now?)

There was a white rose in the New Garden cloister.
(The idol of the man I adored)
Richard, the sea breaks against the sea wall.
("You could undertake that,
When you could not undertake me.")
The plough goes over the soul.
  My Hilary ateliered,
  Femme espaliered, or, woman staked.
  The apricot bears against the south wall
  Daughters too basked at hearth.
  (No more love, no more marriage!)
Which of the chosen ever chose her state?
To hide in love!
Lord, seek Thy servant elsewhere. . . .
  Yet He calls.

I was not invited.
At home at Embly, Wilton, Waverly,
I, sated with invitations,
I, presented to the poor Queen,
I, worthy of the Deaconesses of Kaiserswerth,
Asked by the birthday child to every fête,

I was unwelcome.

The others came.
Two hundred by the shipload,
Jolted from stretchers,
Feverishly crawling up the hill
Through the ice-needled puddles.

I guarded the anteroom
Holding my nurses back, immune
To the cries, the sudden retching spasms, the all
But visible odors. (*Abandon hope all ye who enter here.*)
The mold grew on the walls.

    Blessed are the merciful,
    Says my crowned cross.

Pails of arrowroot, some port . . .
And then, all Balaclava broke loose.
Quick now, old sheets (the dying wait)
Speed, needle! This is no hooped French knot;
A deathbed is required.
    (Where did I yawn
    In the face of the gilt clock
    Defying it to reach 10?)
    Stuff straw for deathbeds, for deathbeds,
    For deathbeds.
    Not one shall die alone.
    I die with each.
    Now hurry to the next lax hand, loose tongue,
    Quick messages for forever.
    Mr. Osborne knelt down for dictation.
    His pencil skirmished among lice.

At last, the chance for a rich and true life.

Outside, the wind rises.
    Wood! the fire dies. . . .
        There is no wood.
    The operating table then. Yes, chop it up.
        (For the operation Mr. Osborne
        Held up the patient with his arms and knee.)

Pen—paper—*vite!*
They demand supplies . . .
Ah ohhh the engine in my head. . . .
Claret and white flour for the Persian adventurer!
    Must I repeat:
Do not
    attach to the cutlets
      (1) rags (2) nails (3) buttons
      . . . surgical scissors

. . . that you can join me on the twenty-seventh
(Crème Harlequin aux Meringues—or dariolettes?)

And again. Please keep:
    a. Toilets covered.
    b. Windows open.
Orderlies: Eat not the rations of those men asleep.
    (*The éclat of this adventure of mine!*)

I dreamed . . .
Compulsive dreaming of the victim.
The rich play in God's garden.
Can they be forgiven?

Their errors gambol scintillating
Under the chandeliers like razors honed.
I murder their heaven,
I, starving, desperate, diseased....
    ("You'll catch something and bring it home.")
Mother, you were willing enough
To part with me to marriage.
No, I must take some things;
They will not be given.
I dream.
    Saints are non-conformists,
    Ladies gone into service,
    Serving ladies with one talent;
    Cast ye the unprofitable servant into outer darkness.

Still-room, pantry, linen room.
Green lists, brown lists, red lists.
Come to me, yearbk of statistics
Of the Deaconesses of Kaiserswerth,
My love, my escape,
My share.
I dreamed of you; now I dream on you:
A hundred baby prayers;
All days garlanded with birthdays, prayers and flowers,
Rye tea. Elevenses: broth without bread:
At last, the chance for a rich and true life.

A girl, desperately fortified in my castle,
The starched pure linen,
Scalded plates, the sanitary air,
The facile word killed soul-ferment.

Six courses starved the spirit.
And I said of laughter, mad,
And of mirth, what is it doing?
I dreamed of all things at man's mercy.

Another boy reached for my hand.

Nurse, keep away. I'm filthy.
My own mother could not touch me.
And I looked sharply down. I was *not*
Wearing my great Paree panjandrum of black velvet.
It was my shawl, my pockets.
     (It is not lady's work.)
I got the burned wing ready.
For eight hundred, sheets and warm food.
"I think I am in heaven," one soldier said.

     Bridget looked up. A lady in black
     Walked up the Lea Hurst drive.
     Miss Flo! our little beauty—
     Come home to die?
     Or come home dead.
     I have looked on Hell.

I wear black for you O British Army.

At night they flare in this soft room:
The long flickering wards,
The muddy uniforms, and sullied faces,
The black, dried, inky blood.

I can never forget.
I stand at the altar of the murdered men
And while I live I fight their cause.

Which of the chosen ever chose her state?
I who looked for some small stanch
Found the world's blood,
Armed with my handkerchief.
Armed with statistics:
Halt! wagons of the heavy artillery.
Cease and desist, wheels of the War Office.
    ("She wept very much.")
I survive them all.
I am sure I did not mean to . . .
No one ever did give up so much to live
Who longed so much to die.
Venez me consoler de n'être pas morte. . . .

. . . Much obliged, Dear George
For your Latin Hey Diddle Diddle
(O God no more love no more marriage.)

Ni lire, ni écrire, ni réfléchir.
I wear black for you O British Army.

    Another boy reached for my hand. . . .

Sir George, thank you
For the Greek Humpty Dumpty.
    (Still He calls.)
Venez me consoler de n'être pas morte.
Venez chez moi on Harley Street.

Bordure de jambon à la Sauvaroff—
Or . . . *quenelles de veau à la Villeroi?*
—The pungent meat pots at Scutari
Seasoned with iron pins, bolts, rusty nails
Tied to each packet.
A skinned sheep lay in the ward all night
To tempt our appetites.
The backed-up drains,
The floor inch-deep in sewage
Seeping under the door.
A thousand diarrheas vs. twenty chamber pots.
Ma'am, I've gone here.

Entry: March 10, 1866. *O!*

  I who could not live
  Without silence and solitude
  Harassed by Parthe's crewel Jesse tree . . .
  (Mother *lied* about the money). . . .
They left my owl locked in the empty house.
In my torment come dreams,
Dreams of Athena who left the Parthenon
To keep house in my pocket,
Forsaken in her feathers,
Her head winding and unwinding,
Eyes blank of me. . . .
Eyes at Scutari following
From cot, from floor, from table, winding-sheet.
For all things at our mercy
Give us grace.

WE ARE THE FRUIT

Tree-in-the-ground
And underneath, a lemon.
The lemon flies the tree,
Has no regrets.
Release is life.

Tree mourns
> It no more needs my thorns
> Flesh of my flesh
> Image of my image
> I cannot follow

Seed flutters
> Let me travel
> Ripening, ripening
> Reflecting the sun
> I know not the tree
> I know not the tree

But anchor to anchor,
Earth to earth, inside you yet
In the garden to come, lemon
Lie your own roots.

THE SKIPPED PAGE

If she stayed on her knees long enough
Maybe somebody would tell her
What she was doing in this house
So long unvisited;
What the beds were doing, made,
That had so long untidily held *them;*
What the sunlight did
Belaying the grimy pane;
And who was that, out there,
Sitting on a child's chair
Near the woodpile, holding a cane,
Facing the winter clouds
With fake fearless gilded eyes.

And she debated, turning her rings,
The dead telephone,
And how she would answer it there,
There where the knife was already in tomorrow
And her plate crying to receive the carcass.

THE WEDDING GUESTS

Just headed out for town
To get the oil can filled,
Had just got to the Southbound Crossing
When I was—
Bidden to the Wedding Feast.
Did I have time to change my overalls?
To shave?
To learn to pick? And sing?
To learn the words? The tune?
    The wife and young ones are at home.
    They'll have no fire tonight.
    And I go down to Hell.

I'd just been down to see
If chance the mail had passed,
And picked a streakèd daisy for my shirt
When this big car pulled up,
This fellow bid me to a spread—
No bluejohn and hard hoecake—
    Seemed like I'd just been laying off to go.

BULLETIN

It's Dr. James gone wild
Who used to save life.
Smite him,
Transfusing the enemy.
Maul him,
Bandaging the firing squad.
Wrest off his gun
And if his arm come with it
And his head
The wet roots twitching thereunto,
The warm roast carved:
Wash the liver
Wash the lights
Breathe life into the lungs
The valves, the wheel chair;
Cherish this white-suited
Uncouth, incurable angel.
Unfold his newspaper,
Unfold his hand,
Run his finger under the commercials:
You grow better
You will not die
It says here:
You will not die
You grow better—
O surgical hands
Hero of the corps
St. Devil

THE DEAD

Suddenly, you
Crossing with the light
Before my windshield.
    Dream,
Come close by me and be warm.
Have, once-more, eyes, eyeballs
Blood vessels . . . pains . . .
Come. Our wars be forgiven us.
No more I crush you
Underneath my wheel,
No more you, intent
On the light, your bent,
Cut me.
Come close, come warm. . . .

The dead are beasts.
We grieve for them
But they don't grieve for us.
They beckon.
    Come here and be cold.
    Lay by those eyes for
    Dreamless dark, those pains
    That beat in pulsing veins.
    By me be bones, be stone.
        In death relax all blocs;
        Shadow and substance lock.

CEMETERY STATUE

Among the leaves and stones
The large white mother cat,
Come home, eyes still
Preoccupied, tail hanging,
But with an angry fret,
Receives the kitten's kiss.
It runs up on tiptoe,
Ears, tail upstretched in bliss—
His mother love,
Her child's indifference met.

PAUSE, IN FLIGHT

Late August. The wind stays awake all night
Thinking of autumn. The crickets wonder
Out loud about the future. . . . Damn the past.
Damn the past. . . . Fall is yonder,
The constellation we are travelling to.
No, we are where it is travelling to
From a distance, a time, long overdue,
Extinguished before the hunter put
The gun over his shoulder. Will these trees
Be the last to receive
This light?
         The crickets, apprehensive,
Give ear. This light, this autumn, this hunter
Comes already dead. Who
Flutters featherless into the leaves?

TO A YOUNG WRITER

If you like love and fame
Shop early, get your shots
Don't spit, and pass with care—
Avoid at all costs
Death, breakdown, despair;
They'll fall on you,
Flock-peck to pieces wounded mouse:
I always thought so—
You know he lacked the drive
It had to come—
Dear friends consign you
To sanitorium, prison, and the pall.
No, keep your chair,
Tuck your wits in,
Say finally
I did outdure them all

But, sir, you know I saw the cops
Remove you from that Bleecker garbage can
Agog with pot.
Remember—analyzing Donne's Sermons
On your Payne Whitney cot?
(Your comments were brilliant, brilliant—
As noted in my journal on the spot.)
All of us heard you rake your wife
For coolness to your whore.
  We wrote it down.
    Laurel becomes a devastated brow.

Don't leave hungry.
Take this bird—eat song.
This wave, drink.

Throw work out the back door
To bleach his bones.
Don't you do it. Play.

Enter night
Unpracticed on vast scales,
On idle rests?
No.
Lap-up the master's saucer—
Eat of this bright flesh—
Drink of this momentary blood—
All thy sins are teggen away, teggen away.

Wake, girl.
Your head is becoming the pillow.
In the other room
Your husband writes a letter.
The mirror is waiting to hold you.
The books at your side
Are reading the years.
The pages tick;
A fuse riffles them.

My condolences. . . .
You're too late too early.

HISTORY PLAN

The weavers pass.
That filled is finished.
Along the canvas
New people rise,
Take stands, and are.
 Fixed in the background,
 Eyes raised,
 My hand arrested fruitlessly,
 My future's stopped.

  When weavers sleep,
  Out of the tapestry
  My nails will creep,
  Pinch up and ravel out
  The well-pulled strings,
  Mottle with spittle,
  The picture loathing—

  Fall, tapestry!
  Ciphers prefer nothing.

COURTESY CALL 1967

I'm back.

But you sleep now,
Who used to be the guardian of the stream.
It needs no guarding now; it's dreaming, too—
Narrower, deeper, sluggish, frosted with leaves.
I think it's comatose.
One used to see, a mile away, wind whip
Your leaves to wrongsideout to sun.
A wind could hardly find this glen today.
That hill was open pasture!
Just now I had to fight my way
To find a spot pine trunks
Were not too logjammed to squeeze through.
It was hard even to find you.
I thought I knew so well.
When the boys dug the swimming hole
They turned the stream;
But it's gone back now,
Their pool washed in,
Their turn filled in with trees—
Trees old (but younger
For trees than they are for boys). . . .

Except that you've grown truly ancient . . .
I? The same.
The same, and elderly.
Like you trapped in some far neglect;
Reflections deepened, dulled,
Our voices out.

VICTORY

Granny Hill—no kin of course—said only sayings:
"Bad luck to drop your comb! Wind-storms come west . . .
"Bad luck to plant a cedar . . . it'll shade your grave."
Something forgotten, her face became obsessed;
She drew a cross-mark in her tracks,
Spat in the cross, before she would turn back.

The Saint girls mimicked her: Bad luck, bad luck!
"Come spend-the-night, girls—We'll eat boiled-butter-and-eggs."
Doctor Will, with a lantern, one fall night
Walked her orchard on dead legs,
And after that she had his power,
A remedy (some, though, severe)
For ingrown nails, chapped hands, consumption;
She talked fire from a swollen hand;
Was never sick herself.
Her face resided in a puckered bonnet;
Her clothes grew on her like a turtle's shell;
Bonnet and skirts smelled faintly henhouse.

Her Sally was a goose,
Shrill and dried up,
And where her baby came from no one knew
Unless it was George Jeans
Who drove the thresh.
But there was harmless Foolish John,
A man's beard, round black hat,
Round stomach like a two-year-old.
The Saint girls ran from him,
His grinning stare, the way he followed them.
He tore things up—old belts, old hats.
An old suspender was his favorite toy.

A moldy shoe found in the gully—Save it for John.
It was excitement,
Like George Jeans, the thresh, and chicken pie—
Three things he stabbed at saying,
Big-eyed, a prophet:
Geor' Jeans! Tresh? Chick' pie!

The Saint girls mimicked him,
Sometimes felt mimicked at the meeting house:
The turtleshell could say the Lord's Prayer backwards:
John sometimes said his words out loud,
Laughed, started for the pulpit.
A little screech from Sally brought him back.
"Whipping's all makes him learn," she'd wail.
They never saw him whipped or misbehave
(But taking off his clothes: "Like a baby—
Don't know no better.")

But one time he was lost three solid days.
Old Mr. Saint went out with them to search.
John! John-n-n!
They scoured the fields and woods all night
Carrying pine torches, calling,
(A lost dog would have come to whistling)
Stopping to stamp out broomstraw caught by sparks.
Three days, and gave him up.
Then found him under David Lee's cow-bridge,
Hovered, teeth chattering,
And led him home across the frozen fields.

Sunday he sat as empty as before.
Lord, whence are Thy hands so rent and torn?
They are pierc'd tonight by many a thorn!
Sally's high voice threw flames on the hymn;
The torches lit up Foolish John's pale face,
So much like hers, like Granny's—a pack of Hills—
And none of the ransom'd ever knew
How deep were the waters crossed
Or how dark the night the Lord passed through
Ere He found His sheep that was lost. . . .

John died first, of bloody flux;
Then Sally caught typhoid.
One morning Granny failed to wake.
Not dead, dried up and blown away, they thought.
Within a month Bess Saint at twilight
Appropriated Granny's shawl and bonnet,
Crept down from Granny's path to where the rest
Were picking berries. They threw their vessels
Far and wide, and to this day say, breathless,
"Bess, know that time—you dressed up like Granny?"

IRONWEED

In poverty of soil,
  in death of summer,
    I bloom—
        decree to bloom—
And in the color of kings.

SIRENS

They trail all travels.
Above the turbo-
Jet: the sirens' wail,
The ambulance
Arriving for one
I never expected
To leave. Below my bunk
Through hull a yard wide
In the land
Of phosphorescence,
Sirens; the attendant
Opens the white door.
Alien country,
Unpacked hotel—
Under the placid
Running bath, sirens,
Expectedly, sirens
Whispering for me.
(She died of internal
Weeping.)
Indestructible
Ears, have mercy.
Siamese partner,
If your heart fail
Shall I not panic?
Sirens have mercy
On my appendaged
Weeping
Lest I dissect us
With one nap.

STET

I can't like the butterfly.
I liked my nymph
Lack-locomotive
Descintillate
Maleloquent.
But the lines flutter off
In clacking print.

TRANSPLANT

Daphne was a real girl
But here is a girl a real tree
Following her god out of the woods,
Trailing torn roots and limp leaves,
Bleeding mud.
    O shells
        husks
            clods
This is no lost sun-dappled girl.
She's a rheum of the woods
Dreaming of snake-cold nest,
Turning your cup to clay,
Sputtering your fire with numbered leaves
From her mortal hood
Ready to chop down Daphne if she could.

ONE NOT DESCENDED

One not descended
From anybody
To those descended
From Mountbattens:

Arise, take hope.
Be queens
Of ascendancy.

Let those in ascendancy
Have dominion
Over those in descendancy.
Ascend, descendants.

O lowly descendants—
Mighty ascendants—

Bury the ladder and scend no more.

FLIGHT

She could not understand it.
By chance twice that day
   turning her head in backward glance,
   she glimpsed a bird perched on her shoulder.

That night, a cry—a devil's squeal,
   a beating at the upstairs window ledge,
   a clawing at the screen in crazed appeal.
Then in the moonlight, wings
   dizzied the eye angling across
   the bed, window to window,
   whirling frantically, and were lost.

      —John, a bird got in our room last night,
      —Oh, Lucy! . . .
         But *A spirit escaped*, she thought,
         And dreaded news.

Next week, two green flies
   fought at the attic window—
Something not freed—
   ensnared in its own flight. . . .
And a letter telling
   of a certain night—
   an old friend met at the airport
   by wife, psychiatrist,
   and plainclothesman. . . .
   "Our genius is doing well."

Bee-legged, bee-spirited, preoccupied,
He stalks the churchyard,
The lifeless earth of hard good-byes:
School chum and cousin! . . .
You wouldn't know me now.
But I'd know you,
    My out-of-date young folks.
That first strange heedlessness was Brother's.
But I was young then, callous—
It was that last one. . . .
    Can it be, grass already?
One night she thought I stood her up.
A flash flood took the bridge;
She waited over there. All kisses
Never really set it right.
To be kept waiting. . . .
    Why do I dally now?
You, fence!—you, road!—
You, spot the ground humps by the holly tree!
How will you exist at twilight,
Without me here?
    Say I stay!
Why can't I say good-bye?
My hand turns for my woods—
My cheek yearns to my sky,
The candle snuffed, the light sped whence it came—
It's hard! and
I decline; in short, won't go.

In the mind's honeycomb are many dreams.
Shall all be sealed, and never a wind whip through?
The sun sets and the fields dissolve.
Now my date waiting in the dark says hungrily
Come to me, life, come to me. I need thee.

RETURN: A PROJECTION

Nobody knows how long it's been
Since we four walked here
Swinging hand-in-hand—

Our world burst outward
Oceans drained in space
That drop of essence at earth's core
Spilled out,
Evaporated—

Till suddenly in shifting chaos-clouds
We mass, re-form,
One moment swinging down the oak-lined road
Towards home and chairs,
Rebirth, a bloodless blood reply,
A foundling on some sill:
We give thee, dominie, back thine eyes.

SONG

Don't go to sleep, I begged.
But a child bending grasses
Under the tamaracks
Could not know
The wear of the field.
In your sleeping face
There was nothing to show
That you remembered me, or cared,
Or would come back.

Don't go to sleep, I cry,
Now gray—but can I know
The stupefaction of all losses?
In your suspended face
No flicker shows
If you remember me, or care,
Or will come back.

ADAPTATION

Innards tied on her apron:
I'll take over.
They sighed. (High time.)
The patient lay motionless
In the same bed in the serene sheets
That had tossed senselessly
All the long voyage.
Is it the plesiosaur I hear?
Is it gruff?
Give me a handkerchief.

With thermometer and melon scoop
Nurse fashions a patient like a boat,
Hull cast indifferently
But feverproof.

ESCAPEE'S DREAM

A cabin in past woods.
Do I live there?
My old schoolmates live round?
And none too glad to have me coming back.
But I'm drawn there.
Running I call for them.
The wind comes flattening my oaks,
Leveling my cabin.
They all have torches, quilts, a hiding spot.

Afterwards, an inmate, I'm allowed
To gather tiger lilies
From their graves.

CONFRONTATION

"I gave Hon her wedding day,
"With silver spoons for favors
"(While you were away).
"Yours are this kind. . . .
"I haven't cleaned them—
"You don't mind?"

    But this is my spoon—mine.
    The silver auction one
    A crater in the plating;
    The other, goldish, galvanized,
    With *U.S.* on the handle—
    Both crusted with wet scouring powder
    Greening. . . .

    Thieves' gifts!
    The hotel towel, the library book,
    The husband feloniously abstracted
    (Your voice in the bedside telephone
    Audible to his wife;
    Wife rose, wept,
    For her institutional item). . . .

    Giver of wedding days
    Giver of dinners
    Giver of spoons sterling
    Return your item to the library
    The Army, the Plaza,
    Not my doorstep, darling!

HIS WISHES

His wishes came wearing war paint
In deft running bursts toward the stockade.

The settlers by the fire listened.
(It's a rough night outside.)

The guard tracking and turning in the snow
Was lulled by a receding rhythm;
The wind threatening and falling back.

Suddenly, without battle, the kill complete.
His torch blazed up a house, a street.
Love, hands tied, staggered off,
All infants threaded on one pale,
All hearth but stone residuum despoiled.

But one pert anti-wish scorned savages,
Sneered at commands,
Refused wild hands until she fell.
The brave, peace-baffled, nurtured her;
By summer, rocked in homespun, war-excelled.

EPITAPH

She lies where doves call, bedded,
From the creek bank; creek bedded, too,
Willow and gum ruched honeysuckle;
The Saint graveyard's neglected.

Her house was screenless; doors stood wide;
Leaves drifted unwatched down the hall;
Hens left warm eggs indoors.
A stray lamb maddened by the scolding floor
Galloping broom to bed to wall to wall
Fell out the back door finally, prayers-answered.

For she was always in the low-grounds
Chopping cotton, or by the orchard
Binding wheat with wheat-strands,
Thinning the corn slips in the new-ground field,
Then home to snatch the coffee pot
Up off the floor (where the baby'd played),
Lay table, before they all got in.

—Kate, this brew's not fit to drink.
    —What? . . .
                Oh Lord.
—Don't cry, Kate
    —But I can't help it
    I never cried for shirtwaists
    Or China cups
    Or crocheted pillow shams. I've not.
    But oh to have it said of me
    She boiled the gosling in the coffee pot . . .
        Poor gosling!

STILL LIFE

What was that?

The petals from a rose
Dropped to the table,
Some spilling on the floor,
Some lying still before
Your photograph.

So, one day now
Down in the grave
They'll settle, the ashes
Of your rapture,

Down underneath where roots
Lose track of seed,
No flowers open and convolve,
No apples madden and exact.

Yet, hard fruit borne on roots,
I descend clinging tuberwise,
Follow still the used bouquet
To keep its company till diggers rise.

A FEW DAYS IN THE SOUTH
IN FEBRUARY
(A Hospitality for S. K. Wightman, 1865)

> *Based on Mr. Wightman's account of his pilgrimage to North Carolina reprinted from family papers in* American Heritage *February 1963.*

I

One ship, one only
One sentry
One grave marked

An old man seeking a battlefield,
I march on the land of the enemy
For my son.
Who will know where he fell?
How take him, taken by the enemy?
How wrest him, young and strong
From war, from peace?

Your Christmas letter descended
Like a Parrot shell and near
Annihilated this home-starved soldier. . . .
Six days before!
Climbing the parapet, a minie ball.
His comrade's flask implored declining lips.

The battlefield stretches south.
Is it salt-marsh birds—
Or dead soldiers whistling?
Nightmare or real madness?
I stumble over dead grass locked in ice.

47

This alien wind blows sand
Not southern; arctic sand peppers
My flowing eyes and face.
I hear my wild voice singing hymns;
Feel tears like death-throes shake me,
Then breath gives out and I sit down to rest.
The salt wind roughs sand-wounds.
The eye calls, *Edward*. . . .
Answer, only those wind-borne birds.
Expanse of sea and marsh.
Expanse of dunes.

I hail the single soldier strolling near.
We two meet in an empty world.
    (Surely the bounds of fate,
     A grim tale's magic.)
"Graves from the battle of January 15?"
"On that knoll, sir."

    Surely the bounds of our lives
    Are fixed by our Creator.
    One marked, one only,
    The pine-stave written on in lamp-black.
    My trembling spectacles give time for magic:
     Sergt Major
       3rd NYV
         E.K. Wightman

The darling of his sisters, mother
His steady eye, good sense
His quiet dreams
It seems I may spend out my years
Beside the spot.

I walk away,
Return and weep again.

Again I try to go on with my plan,
Set out for General Terry's—
Come back to him.

Three times I leave and
Stay to mourn.

> So, thanking God for His
> Mercy and goodness to me—
> Only one grave marked.
> Surely the bounds of our lives

Take up the body now?
Only a pine coffin? Ah.
At some future time. . . .
With one of lead. . . .

Gentlemen, I must say
Without intending to offend that
(If it be not counter to God's will)
I will never leave Federal Point
Without Edward's body.

"If we had salt and rosin. . . .
"Things unsettled. . . ."
    Only to wait,
    Thanking God for His mercy and goodness:
    One ship, one only.
    One sentry,
    One grave marked.

    On the sealing of coffins. . . .
Salt in supply.
Tentcloth, none. No pitch nor rosin.

III

(Surely the bounds of fate,
A grim tale's magic)
    No pitch   no rosin
Here near the tidewater is a knoll of sand.
I loiter,
Led by—the devil despair?
Godmother in disguise?
The hand of God?
    Take this fragment of a pick-ax
    And look there near the tidewater.
        Hans, or Abraham, obey.

To my astonishment. . . .
A barrel of rosin
There buried in the sand.
      Tears, thanking, etc.

I take the load upon my back
Struggling through deep sand
      (*Especially as . . . not at that time*
      In good health and not for years
      Subject to so great exposure)

Near nightfall, greatly fatigued,
I drift into a German fairy tale:
      Pity the sorrows of a poor old man
      Whose trembling limbs have borne him to your door. . . .

      "Orderly, take your horse and another;
      "Go with this gentleman to the Point."

And so aboard the *Montauk* for the night.

IV

Needing what you don't want is hell.
A need for pitch, for sealing-black. . . .
Again stand at the magic spot
The Cape Fear's tide,
Conjure a barrel grounded in the shallows
Delightful as the ark in Pharaoh's flags
Delightful as the babe to Levi's house,
This coffin-gift.

The tide gone out, the barrel turns to staves--
Staves thick-pitched inside.
     Thanking God, etc. . . . .

Beside the joiner's bench
I steady planks, his bed,
Give from my hand the separate coffin nails,
     Thanking God,

                        v
A tent-cloth, a detail of men,
A hollow in the sand, a fire,
Pitch and a little rosin in a pot.
It bubbles smackingly.
We frost the coffin and pitch tight the box,
Swab black the tent-cloth.

Unbidden blue coats straggle round
To meet my son.
I watch each salt of sand
On each gross shovel
Each inch to forty-eight,
Down to the end of miracles.

He lies half-turned,
His braided collar up
Against the elements (now chiefly earth)
Cape folded over face.
     Face . . . speeding from face to skull.
     (*The teeth appeared very prominent.*)

What has your plum-pudding to do with me?
Ah, my friends, thus it was with the captain
In ancient times, when afar off he gazed
At the smoking ruins
Of the beloved city of his birth
Burned by a barbarous enemy

In enemy land
Who mourns burned cities?
—Ruin!
Consider the holes made by the ball.
The hands, you judge, are very like. . . .
    ("Ah, can ye doubt?" asks one rough man,
    "For sure now, he greatly resembles ye")
    Face, white and swollen;
    Eyes, somehow injured.
    The wreck of our anticipations
    His love for me. . . .
    His Virgil parody. . . .
    "A favorite with the men"

        A puzzle, one set out so late
        Has overshot into eternity
        And left me plodding on.

At last I let them.
They wind the cloth about him.
And I, mounting, whip to Fort Lamb
Driven by the hammers.

Some days are pages ragtorn from hell.
Yet on this cruellest day night came.
Aboard the *Montauk*, water-rocked,
I slept, slept peacefully,
As if we two
Slept in our beds at home.

V I

His corpse recaptured from the enemy,
I brought him back where he was born
To that address his letters came.
 ("*To all—Dear Father Mother Fred*
   Abbie and Jim Chas
     Mary Ell and
      Babies")
To services appropriately grave.
There lie in peace till Morning.
The sent-out child lies harvested.
The stone doves peck.

 My watch ticks in my waistcoat.
 My *News* waits by the window.
 Snow falls
  I believe that the bounds of our lives
  Are fixed by our Creator
  And we cannot pass them.
  The Lord gives and the Lord takes away
  Blessed be the name of the Lord.

54

ENVOY

better than any of you, poems,
are the eyes
that scribble themselves
    across the sky
    out the window
    before dinner just as the doorbell rings
    across the ceiling touched by carlights
    at night when there are too many people to wake